ORGAN CONCERTO

B♭ major
Opus 4/2

Edited by/Herausgegeben von
Peter Williams

Ernst Eulenburg Ltd

London · Mainz · Madrid · New York · Paris · Tokyo · Toronto · Zürich

G. F. HANDEL

Organ Concertos, Op. IV

Handel's Op. IV is not only the first and best-known set of organ-concertos ever published but itself established a *genre*. The English Organ Concerto as a whole has more recently received attention elsewhere[1], and from modern editions, including a forthcoming volume in *Musica Britannica*, it can be seen how the *genre* eventually encompassed concertos for the small theatre-organs playing in the intervals between acts of oratorios, for the instruments in the band-stands of the Pleasure Gardens of London and elsewhere, for church organs at special celebration or dedication Services, and for concert-hall organs playing symphonic concertos at a later period.

It is to the first of these categories that Handel's Op. IV belongs, and though the organ-writing of the later concerto Op. VII No. 1 may suggest performance outside a theatre (see foreword, Eulenberg Edition Nos. 1291–6), it was as oratorio interlude-music – or, perhaps more accurately, as music prefacing the start of an Act in an oratorio – that all of Handel's organ concertos seem to have originated. That was not so with the first known set published by a composer other than Handel, viz. Henry Burgess's *Six Concertos* (c1741), which arose from or for his duties as Pleasure-Garden organist; nor with the sets soon published for a market that had blossomed overnight, e.g. J. A. Hasse's *Six Concertos* (c1741 – imported harpsichord concertos) and John Stanley's *Six Concertos* (c1745 – arrangements of string concertos). That Handel's Op. IV has movements or themes found elsewhere in the composer's work[2] does not detract from its special position as a collection of works written or compiled (a) as interlude-music for specific oratorios, (b) to be played by their composer himself as an extra and well-publicized attraction, and (c) as originators of a *genre* in England. Nor does the fitful tradition on the continent of Europe for concertos or single movements with solo organ – a tradition spanning Venetian *ospedale* concertos to the full-fledged works of classical Hapsburg composers – affect these special claims of Handel's Op. IV, though it does perhaps explain how Handel came to construct interlude-concertos in the London theatres. Perhaps it was in Rome, and certainly in Italy, that he heard or conceived the idea of giving the ubiquitous *continuo* organ some *obbligato* passages in a ritornello movement, roughly corresponding to the solo passages played by a violin or a string trio in the conventional concerto grosso. The single-movement *Sonata* in *Il Trionfo del Tempo* (1707) is of this kind, and it is more likely, judging from the organ-figuration and keyboard style, that this *Sonata*

---

[1] e.g. C. Cudworth, 'The English Organ Concerto', *The Score* 8 (1953) 51ff; A. Hutchings, 'The English Concerto with or for Organ', *The Musical Quarterly* 47 (1961) 195ff; P. Williams, 'Händel und die englische Orgelmusik', *Händel-Jahrbuch* 12 (1966) 51ff; N. K. Nielsen, 'Handel's Organ Concertos reconsidered', *Dansk Aarborg for Musikforskning* 3 (1963) 3–26. The best available description of the musical background to Handel's organ concertos is in Stanley Sadie's *Handel Concertos* (BBC Music Guides, 1972)

[2] In view of at least one work-in-progress on Handel's self-borrowings, no provisional list has been attempted in this edition.

IV

reflects Italian organ-playing in secular or semi-secular contexts than that it represents organ-music of a kind Handel would have heard or played in Halle or even Hamburg. That in *Il Trionfo* the Sonata is followed by a recitative, and the recitative by an aria with important passages for organ, is also important evidence for Handel's conception of organ concertos, since the overall plan of these three movements then corresponds closely to the structure of, e.g. the Concerto Op. IV No. 2 in B flat major.

Although the dates of Op. IV have been better established by such modern writers as Sadie (see note 1), the general picture as drawn by Burney[3] remains true:

> . . . in 1732, *Esther* . . . in March, 1733, *Deborah* . . . It was during these early performances of Oratorios, that Handel first gratified the public by the performance of Concertos on the Organ, a species of Music wholly of his own invention (*a*), in which he usually introduced an extempore fugue, a diapason-piece, or an adagio, manifesting not only the wonderful fertility and readiness of his invention, but the most perfect accuracy and neatness of execution (*b*).
>
> (*a*) Rameau's *Livre de Pièces de Clavecin en Concerts*, did not appear till 1741.
>
> (*b*) The favourite movemement, at the end of his second organ-concerto, was long called the *Minuet in the Oratorio of Esther*, from the circumstance of its having been first heard in the concerto which he played between the parts of that Oratorio.

The success of these performances is attested by various sources from the 1730s, such as the newspaper report which called Nos. 2 and 3 'inimitable', or the newspaper advertisements (*London Daily Post*, March 1735) for *Esther* at Covent Garden, where were promised 'several New Additional Songs; likewise two new Concerto's on the Organ'. Obviously, Handel was a player able to stir, even bewitch an audience; according to Burney (*ibid*), he opened the theatre organ in Oxford

> in such a manner as astonished every hearer. The late Mr Michael Christian Festing, and Dr Arne, who were present, both assured me, that neither themselves, nor any one else of their acquaintance, had ever before heard such extempore, or such premeditated playing, on that or any other instrument.

That was in 1733, the year claimed by Burney to have seen the first concerto.

Why Handel waited some years before publishing an organ concerto is unclear; such delay was not uncommon for instrumental works at the period, and in any case he seems to have composed them only spasmodically, perhaps one or two per oratorio season. In 1738, No. 2 was published in a simple, two-stave arrangement in *The Lady's Entertainment . . . to which is prefix'd the celebrated Organ Concerto*. Whether this prompted the full publication of Op. IV in the autumn of 1738 (solo part in October, instrumental parts in December) is not known, but Walsh, who published both, added (or had added, or was asked to add) the remark that an earlier (two-stave) edition was 'spurious and incorrect'. What this earlier edition was is not known. Only two years later, Op. IV was re-issued and, in one or other edition, has been ever since. Probably

---

[3] C. Burney, *An Account of the Musical Performances . . . in Commemoration of Handel* (London, 1785) 23

in no year since they were published have these concertos been unobtainable in the music shops of London, which cannot be said of most, if any, other English organ-music.

One element in Burney's description is puzzling: that in the concertos 'he usually introduced an extempore fugue, a diapason, or an adagio'[4]. Does this apply to Op. IV or only to Op. VII, where *ad libs*, both of solo ritornello episodes and of whole movements, are specified and even cued? Is Burney's remark more than a de-embroidered version of the passage in Hawkins's *History*[5] concerning his way of beginning a concerto with the kind of movement already very popular amongst English organists at the time:

> a voluntary movement on the diapasons, which stole on the ear in a slow and solemn progression; the harmony close wrought, and as full as could possibly be expressed . . . This kind of prelude was succeeded by the concerto itself . . .

And was Hawkins speaking of performances he himself may have witnessed – presumably of the concertos later than Op. IV – or of the earlier concertos, for which his evidence was probably hearsay? It is difficult to believe that in Op. IV – even allowing for Burney's escape-clause 'usually' – Nos. 1, 3 and 5 would have been prefaced by an improvized solo movement, 'slow, solemn, close wrought'. One cannot be certain what the composer may have done in practice, particularly as the published concertos were prepared specifically for their publication and hence for sale to players who did not want to read *ad lib* signs as soon as they opened their copy. But if, for example, the *Ouverture* at the beginning of No. 2 was prefaced by such a prelude, it can only have been as a means of preparing an audience more restless in the interludes between Acts than it was during the Acts themselves. Nor perhaps can Hawkins's fulsome praise of Handel's organ-playing be fully understood today, when close acquaintance with the organ-music of his German contemporaries has familiarized organists with the complex counterpoint, intricate form and major technical demands of which the organ is capable:

> As to his performance on the organ, the powers of speech are so limited, that it is almost a vain attempt to describe it otherwise than by its effects . . . and his amazing command of the instrument, the fullness of his harmony, the grandeur and dignity of his style, the copiousness of his imagination, and the fertility of his invention were qualities that absorbed every inferior attainment.

Yet obviously Handel must have had an extraordinary panache, rather comparable to the genius of the Italian violinist of that and other periods, one imagines. To over-value 'complex counterpoint, intricate form and major technical demands' is to fall into the same error as those writers on J. S. Bach in the later 18th century who could never understand how Handel could ever be properly compared with their own idol.

The organ required for these concertos is the English chamber organ of seven or eight stops, a type known from Handel's letter to Jennens of 1749 and from

---

[4] 'a diapason-piece, or an adagio' is unclear as to punctuation but probably means 'a piece, i.e. an adagio prelude, for the two diapasons'

[5] J. Hawkins, *A General History of the Science and Practice of Music* (Novello edn., 1853) 912

VI

other instruments existing then and later in London theatres and gardens. Because of gentle English voicing and a disregard for Mixture stops, these organs were generally softer and less splendid than comparable instruments with the same number of stops in other countries.

Letter to Jennens, 1749 (O E. Deutsch, *Handel: a documentary Biography* (London, 1955), pp675-6)	Covent Garden Theatre (early 19th-cent. ms ed C W Pearce, *Notes on English Organs* (London, n d), p160) Built by Jordan (burnt 1808)	Drury Lane Theatre (source as Covent Garden, p161) Built by Byfield & Green, 1769 (burnt 1809)
GG-d''' ('full octave')	GG-d''' (55 notes, no GG sharp)	I GG-e''' (no GG sharp) II c'-e'''
		I (*Great*)
Open Diapason 8 (metal throughout)	Open Diapason 8	Open Diapason 8 (from tenor G only)
Stop Diapason 8	Stop Diapason 8	Stop Diapason 8
Principal 4	Principal 4	Principal 4
Flute 4		Flute 4
Twelfth 2⅔	Twelfth 2⅔	
Fifteenth 2	Fifteenth 2	Fifteenth 2
Tierce 1⅗	Tierce 1⅗	
		Sesquialtera III
	Trumpet 8	Trumpet 8
		II (*Swell*)
		Open Diapason 8
		Principal 4
		Cornet III
		Hautboy 8

That the 'Old Theatre Royal, Covent Garden' specification as given in c1810 contains no Flute stop called for in Op. IV or in the organ-part to *Alexander's Feast* could mean (a) that his organ was not there in c1735-40, (b) that Handel meant to indicate only a general effect (e.g. that the 8.8.4 registration for Op. IV No. 4 Andante is low-pitched and discreet because of the high *tessitura* of the solo line), or (c) that Handel did not have this organ in mind. Other conjectures are possible; but either way, the presence or absence of a Flute stop has little bearing on the type of organ required, which is clear enough. Whether Handel ever had an organ of two manuals for his theatre concertos is not known; if he did, it would probably have dated only after Op. IV – perhaps for *Saul* or for the concerto Op. VII No. 1 or for a (later?) version of Op. IV No. 3 (first movement), in which cases it would have been natural for a central German to think of pedals and two manuals as necessary for each other. That there were no reeds in Handel's scheme is, in the composer's words, 'because they are continually wanting to be tuned, which in the country is very inconvenient', though not in London's West End. Handel's stipulation in his letter to Jennens that the Open Diapason be metal throughout supports the description of his playing low sustained Diapason music, for which a good metal bass is vital. The instrument presented by this tonal picture contrasts strongly with the little organs the composer would have known in Germany[6]; in almost every

---

[6] See e.g. P. Williams, 'A newly restored Handel Organ', *Musical Times* 1606 (1976) 1031-33

respect – tone of individual ranks, position in the building, acoustics of the building, pitch, tuning and compass of the organ – the two kinds of instruments had nothing in common. Much more like the London theatre organ was the larger Italian *positivo*, and it cannot be coincidence that the organ-writing found in the *Il Trionfo* movements related both to Italian keyboard-music and Italian organs, thus anticipating Op. IV.

Conforming also to Italian practice would be Handel's registration: the Open Diapason+Stopped Diapason+Flute of Op. IV No. 4, and also the Open Diapason+Principal+Stopped Diapason+Flute of the organ part for the Ouverture to *Alexander's Feast* (ms keyboard score, R.M. 19.a.1). This latter suggests that no high ranks were drawn even in *tutti forte* movements. Presumably it was because of the limited nature of the theatre organs that the basso continuo part for the chorus 'There let the pealing organ blow' in *L'Allegro* was specified by Handel for 'Org. etc et Basson Grosso' (ms R.M. 20.d.5); what he wanted was a German pedal-reed. The quasi-baroquery of modern registrations, quite apart from the use of organs totally out of character, reflects a serious misunderstanding of the origins and context of Handel's organ concertos.

For the present edition, I have followed Chrysander (*Händel-Gesellschaft* 28) and Matthäi (*Hällische Händel-Ausgabe* IV/2) in taking regard of both ms scores and the first-edition printed parts, though collating them more completely than either earlier editor. I have kept the order as found in Walsh's first edition, although it is more likely that the order of composition is 3–2–5–4–6–1. Presumably the published order was approved by the composer. In Op. VII there is often doubt about (a) the contents of each concerto, (b) the order of movements, (c) the scoring for basses, (d) the scoring for wind and strings, and (e) the style, type and length of the *ad lib* solo passages or movements for organ; rarely is there any doubt about any of these elements in Op. IV, although there are some puzzling *ad lib* signs and some uncertain woodwind scoring. Every movement in the Basso part is figured; but who figured the parts, and why the organ-bass of certain movements is also figured in Walsh's keyboard score, are uncertain. Perhaps harmonies or at least a third part were added to these movements only; perhaps they were added to *all* movements, particularly slow movements, when convenient or discreet; perhaps the figures are evidence of a second keyboard instrument used for *continuo* work; perhaps they are merely indications of the harmonies implied by or worked out in the other lines. Of these, the first or last is the most likely. However, since the orchestral bass is also generally figured, there may be further evidence here that a second keyboard instrument ought to play, were it not that that period seems often to have liked figures to be added purely as an indication of the harmonies implied by or realized in the other parts. Either way, scoring indications for both Nos. 4 and 6 (see notes to those concertos) show the composer to have expected a *continuo* harpsichord to play in the first and a *continuo* organ to play in the second. The printed solo part itself incorporates a two-stave reduction of the ritornello music (marked 'tutti') and of the 'senza Org.' passages as well as the soloist's part proper, marked 'Org. solo'. Some sections and movements are figured in the solo part, others not; this more

VIII

probably reflects the state of the engraver's copy (or his reading of it) rather than a consistent policy on the part of the composer.

This edition owes much to Mr Anthony Hicks, who gave much useful and valuable advice, to Dr William Gudger, who kindly placed his dissertation *The Organ Concertos of Handel* (Yale, 1973) at my disposal, and to Mr Brian Bowen, who saw the edition through the press.

Peter Williams, 1978

G. F. HÄNDEL
Orgelkonzerte Op. IV

Die in Op. IV gesammelten Werke von Händel sind nicht nur die frühesten und bekanntesten Orgelkonzerte, die gedruckt worden sind, sie haben auch als Vorbild für ein ganzes Genre gedient. Die Bedeutung des englischen Orgelkonzerts im Allgemeinen ist in letzter Zeit anderswo behandelt worden[1], und aus Ausgaben unserer Zeit, worunter sich ein Band der *Musica Britannica* befindet, der demnächst erscheinen wird, lässt sich ersehen, wie dieses Genre allmählich Konzerte für kleine Theaterorgeln, die in den Pausen zwischen den Akten von Oratorien spielten, einbezogen hat, sowie Konzerte für Instrumente in den Musikpavillons der Londoner und anderer Vergnügungsparks, für Kirchenorgeln bei besonderen Festlichkeiten oder Weiheakten, und schliesslich für Orgeln in Konzertsälen, die zu einer späteren Zeit sinfonische Konzerte spielten.

Händels Op. IV gehört zu der ersten dieser Kategorien, und obwohl der Stil in der das später entstandene Konzert Op. VII Nr. 1 für die Orgel gesetzt ist, darauf hinzudeuten scheint, dass es für eine Aufführung ausserhalb eines Theaters gedacht war (vgl. hierzu das Vorwort zur Eulenburg-Ausgabe Nr. 1291-6), ist anzunehmen, dass alle Orgelkonzerte von Händel als Zwischenaktmusik für Oratorien entstanden sind – genauer gesagt, als Musik, die den Anfang eines Aktes in einem Oratorium einleiteten. Dies war jedoch bei dem ersten bekannten Satz von Konzerten, die von einem anderen Komponisten als Händel veröffentlicht worden ist, nicht der Fall, nämlich bei den *Six Concertos* (c. 1741) von Henry Burgess, die aus dessen Pflichten als Organist im Vergnügungspark, oder für seine Konzerte dort, entstanden sind, ebensowenig wie bei den Sätzen, die bald für einen Markt herausgegeben wurden, der sozusagen übernacht entstanden war, wie z.B. J. A. Hasses *Six Concertos* (eingeführte Cembalokonzerte, c. 1741) und John Stanleys *Six Concertos* (Transkriptionen von Streicherkonzerten, c. 1745). Die Tatsache, dass in Händels Op. IV Sätze stehen, die auch in seinen anderen Werken zu finden sind[2], verringert nicht seine spezielle Bedeutung (a) als eine Sammlung von Werken, die jeweils als Zwischenaktmusik für besondere Oratorien geschrieben oder zusammengestellt worden sind, (b) als eine vom Komponisten selbst gespielte, gut angekündigte Attraktion als Zugabe, und (c) als ein in England traditionsschaffendes Werk. Genausowenig beeinträchtigt die unstete Tradition von Konzerten oder einzelnen Sätzen mit der Orgel als Soloinstrument auf dem

---

[1] wie z.B. C. Cudworth, 'The English Organ Concerto', *The Score* 8 (1953) S. 51 ff.; A. Hutchings, 'The English Concerto with or for Organ', *The Musical Quarterly* 47 (1961) S. 195 ff.; P. Williams, 'Händel und die englische Orgelmusik', *Händel-Jahrbuch* 12 (1966) S. 51 ff.; N. K. Nielsen, 'Handel's Organ Concertos reconsidered', *Dansk Aarbog for Musikforskning* 3 (1963) S. 3–16.
Die zur Zeit aufschlussreichsten Ausführungen über die näheren musikalischen Umstände, die Händels Orgelkonzerten zugrunde liegen, stehen in Stanley Sadies *Handel Concertos* (BBC Music Guides 1972)

[2] Da gegenwärtig mindestens eine Abhandlung über die von Händel aus eigenen Werken entlehnte Stellen in Arbeit ist, wurde in der vorliegenden Ausgabe keine vorläufige Liste solcher Stellen angegeben.

europäischen Festland – eine Tradition, die von den venezianischen *Ospedale-* Konzerten bis zu den vollentwickelten Werken der klassischen Habsburger Komponisten reicht – auf keine Weise den besonderen Anspruch, den Händels Op. IV erheben kann, obwohl dadurch vielleicht erklärt werden könnte, wie er dazu kam, Zwischenaktkonzerte in die Vorstellungen Londoner Theater einzufügen. Vielleicht hat Händel in Rom, aber sicher in Italien, etwas gehört, oder es war ihm etwas eingefallen, das ihn dazu brachte, der ewigen Continuo-Orgel einige obligate Passagen in einem Ritornellosatz zu geben, die ungefähr den Solopassagen einer Geige, oder eines Streichertrios, in einem konventionellen Concerto grosso entsprechen. Die einsätzige *Sonata Il Trionfo del Tempo* (1707) gehört auch zu dieser Kategorie, und auf Grund der Orgelfiguration und dem Satz für die Manuale, ist anzunehem, dass diese *Sonata* eher vom italienischen Orgelspiel bei weltlichen oder teilweise weltlichen Gelegenheiten beeinflusst worden ist, als von der Orgelmusik, die Händel in Halle oder sogar in Hamburg gehört haben mag. Weiterhin ist es ein wesentliches Merkmal von der Vorstellung, die Händel sich vom Orgelkonzert gemacht hat, dass in *Il Trionfo* nach der *Sonata* ein Rezitativ, und nach dem Rezitativ eine Arie mit solistischen Orgelpassagen folgt, weil die Gesamtanlage dieser drei Sätze ziemlich genau der Struktur eines Konzerts wie z.B. Op. IV Nr. 2 in B-Dur entspricht.

Obgleich die Entstehungsdaten des Op. IV von modernen Autoren wie Sadie (vgl. Fussnote 1) mit grösserer Genauigkeit festgelegt worden sind, hat der von Burney wiedergegebene allgemeinere Eindruck bleibende Bedeutung[3]:

> . . . 1732, *Esther* . . . im März, 1733, *Deborah* . . . Während dieser frühen Aufführungen von Oratorien erfreute Händel das Publikum zum ersten Mal durch die Wiedergabe von Orgelkonzerten, welche eine Musikgattung darstellten, die ganz seiner Erfindung zu verdanken war (*a*). Gewöhnlich spielte er dazu eine improvisierte Fuge, ein mit den Diapasonstimmen gespieltes Stück, oder ein Adagio, worin er nicht allein den Reichtum seiner stets gegenwärtigen Einfallskraft manifestierte, sondern auch dabei die vollkommenste Genauigkeit und Sauberkeit in der Ausführung bewies (*b*).
>
> (*a*) Rameaus Buch *Livre de Pieces de Clavecin en Concerts* erschien erst 1741.
>
> (*b*) Der beliebteste Satz, am Ende seines zweiten Orgelkonzerts, wurde lange als das *Menuett im Oratorium Esther* bezeichnet, weil es zum ersten Mal als Teil des Konzerts zur Aufführung kam, das er zwischen den Akten des Oratoriums gespielt hatte.

Der Erfolg dieser Aufführungen wird durch verschiedene Quellen aus den dreissiger Jahren des achtzehnten Jahrhunderts bestätigt, wie z.B. durch den Bericht einer Zeitung, der Nr. 3 und 4 als ‚unvergleichlich‘ bezeichnete, oder durch die Inserate für *Esther* in Covent Garden (*London Daily Post*, März 1735), in welchen ‚einige Neue Zusätzliche Lieder, und gleichfalls zwei neue Konzerte für die Orgel‘ angekündigt wurden. Offensichtlich hatte Händel die Fähigkeit, das Publikum durch sein Spielen anzuregen, ja zu faszinieren. Wie Burney berichtet (*ib.*), weihte er die Theaterorgel in Oxford

> auf eine Art und Weise ein, dass jeder Zuhörer erstaunt war. Der verstorbene Mr Michael Christian Festing, und Dr Arne, die beide zugegen waren, haben

---

[3] C. Burney, *An Account of the Musical Performances . . . in Commemoration of Handel* (London, 1785) S. 23

mir versichert, dass weder sie selbst, noch irgendwer in ihrer Bekanntschaft jemals derartige Improvisationen, oder ein so von vornherein durchdachtes Spiel, auf diesem oder irgendeinem anderen Instrument, gehört hatten.

Das war im Jahre 1733, in dem Burney behauptet, das erste Konzert gesehen zu haben.

Wie es dazu kam, dass Händel ein paar Jahre verstreichen liess, bevor er ein Orgelkonzert herausgab, ist nicht klar. Derartige Verzögerungen in der Drucklegung waren damals bei Instrumentalwerken nicht ungewöhnlich, und es scheint jedenfalls, dass er sie nur mit Abständen dazwischen komponiert hat, also vielleicht nur ein oder zwei Konzerte für jede Oratoriensaison. Nr. 2 wurde 1738 als einfaches Arrangement auf zwei Systemen in der *Unterhaltung der Dame . . . welcher das berühmte Orgelkonzert vorangeht* veröffentlicht. Ob dadurch die vollständige Drucklegung des Op. IV im Herbst 1738 (die Solostimme im Oktober, und die der anderen Instrumente im Dezember) veranlasst wurde, ist nicht bekannt, aber Walsh, der für beide Ausgaben verantwortlich war, fügte die Bemerkung hinzu (oder hatte sie hinzugefügt, oder war darum gebeten worden, sie hinzuzufügen), dass eine frühere Ausgabe (auf zwei Systemen) ‚unecht und fehlerhaft' war. Um welche frühere Ausgabe es sich dabei handelte, ist nicht bekannt. Schon zwei Jahre später erschien Op. IV in einer neuen Auflage, und seither sind immer wieder neue Auflagen in verschiedenen Ausgaben erschienen. Es hat wohl seit der ersten Auflage kein Jahr gegeben, in dem diese Konzerte in den Londoner Musikläden unerhältlich waren. Das gleiche kann von den wenigsten anderen, wenn überhaupt von irgendeinem der englischen Orgelwerke gesagt werden.

Eins ist in Burneys Beschreibung rätselhaft, und zwar die Stelle über die Konzerte, in welchen er ‚gewöhnlich eine improvisierte Fuge, ein mit den Diapasonstimmen gespieltes Stück, oder ein Adagio' vortrug[4]. Bezieht sich das auf Op. IV, oder nur auf Op. VII, in dem *ad lib.* Passagen für Ritornello-Episoden und für ganze Sätze verlangt, ja sogar angegeben werden? Ist Burneys Bemerkung mehr als eine ernüchterte Fassung der Stelle in der *History* von Hawkins[5], die beschreibt, wie er ein Konzert mit jener Art von Satz begann, wie sie damals schon bei englischen Organisten beliebt geworden war:

eine Fantasie mit den Diapasonstimmen, die sich einem mit langsamem feierlichem Gang ins Gehör schlich; die Harmonie war dicht verflochten und so reich, wie sie sich nur ausdrücken lässt . . . Auf diese Art von Präludium folgte dann das Konzert selbst . . .

Und bezog sich Hawkins dabei auf Aufführungen, denen er selbst beigewohnt haben mag – wobei es sich vermutlich um die später als Op. IV geschriebenen Konzerte handelt – oder auf die früheren Konzerte, bei denen er sich wahrscheinlich auf Berichte Anderer gestützt hat? Es ist kaum vorstellbar, dass in

---

[4] ‚ein mit Diapasonstimmen gespieltes Stück, oder ein Adagio' ist, der Interpunktation wegen, unklar, bedeutet aber vermutlich ‚ein Stück, d.h. ein Adagio-Präludium für die beiden Diapasonstimmen'.

[5] J. Hawkins, *A General History of the Science and Practice of Music* (Novello-Ausgabe, 1853) S. 912

Op. IV – selbst wenn man Burneys Rücktrittsklausel ‚gewöhnlich' berücksichtigt – vor Nr. 1, 3 und 5 ein ‚langsamer, feierlicher, dicht verflochtener' improvisierter Solosatz gestanden hat. Es lässt sich nicht mit Gewissheit sagen, was der Komponist praktisch beim Spielen getan hat, schon allein deshalb nicht, weil die gedruckten Konzerte speziell für den Verkauf an Spieler eingerichtet wurden, die beim Öffnen ihrer Exemplare nicht gleich irgendwelche *ad lib.* Angaben vorfinden wollten. Wenn jedoch ein solches Präludium z.B. vor der *Ouverture*, zu Anfang von Nr. 2, gespielt wurde, so kann der Grund dafür nur darin liegen, dass damit ein Publikum, das sich zwischen den Akten unruhiger verhielt als während der Akte, in die rechte Stimmung gebracht werden sollte. Ebensowenig mag das übertriebene Lob, das Hawkins dem Orgelspiel Händels spendete, heute ganz verständlich sein, da eine genauere Kenntnis der Orgelmusik seiner deutschen Zeitgenossen, die heutigen Organisten mit dem komplizierten Kontrapunkt, der verzwickten Form und den hauptsächlichen technischen Ansprüchen, denen die Orgel gerecht werden kann, vertraut gemacht hat:

> Was sein Orgelspiel anbelangt, so sind die Ausdrucksmöglichkeiten der Sprache so begrenzt, dass man sich fast vergebens bemühen würde, es anders als durch seine Wirkung zu beschreiben . . . und seine erstaunliche Beherrschung des Instruments, die Fülle seiner Harmonien, die Grossartigkeit und Würde seines Stils, der Reichtum seiner Fantasie und die Fruchtbarkeit seiner Einfallskraft waren Eigenschaften, die jede geringere Leistung zunichte machten.

Dennoch muss Händel ausserordentlich brilliant auf das Publikum gewirkt haben, ähnlich, könnte man sich vorstellen, wie die genialen italienischen Geiger seiner und anderer Zeiten. Den ‚komplizierten Kontrapunkt, die verzwickte Form und die hauptsächlichen technischen Ansprüche' übermässig zu bewerten, heisst, dieselben Fehler begehen, wie jene Autoren des späteren achtzehnten Jahrhunderts, die nie begreifen konnten, wie man Händel überhaupt mit ihrem Idol, J. S. Bach, vergleichen konnte.

Das für diese Konzerte erforderliche Instrument war die englische Kammerorgel mit sieben oder acht Registern, und der Typus diese Instruments ist uns durch Händels Brief an Jennens aus dem Jahre 1749 bekannt*, sowie durch andere Instrumente, die damals, wie auch später, in den Londoner Theatern und Vergnügungsparks zu finden waren. Wegen ihres sanften englischen Klangs, und der Ablehnung der Mixturregister, waren diese Orgeln im allgemeinen leiser und weniger prächtig als vergleichbare Instrumente mit derselben Anzahl von Registern in anderen Ländern.

Die Tatsache, dass die genaueren Angaben von *c.* 1810 für die Orgel im ‚alten Theatre Royal, Covent Garden' kein ‚Flute stop' enthielt, das für Op. IV, oder für die Orgelstimme in *Alexander's Feast* vorgeschrieben war, könnte bedeuten, dass (a) diese Orgel *c.* 1735–40 noch nicht da war, dass (b) Händel nur einen allgemeinen Effekt andeuten wollte (d.h., dass die für Op. IV Nr. 4, Andante, angegebene Registration 8.8.4 tief lag und, wegen der hohen Lage der Solostimme diskret blieb), oder dass (c) Händel dabei nicht an diese

---

* Vgl. die das Orgelwerk betreffende Angabe im englischen Vorwort S.VI.

bestimmte Orgel gedacht hatte. Andere Möglichkeiten wären ebenfalls denkbar. Wie dem auch sei, das Vorhandensein oder Fehlen eines ‚Flute stops‘ hat offensichtlich wenig mit dem speziellen Typ des Instruments zu tun, das hier verlangt war. Es ist nicht ermittelt worden, ob Händel je für die Aufführungen seiner Konzerte in Theatern eine Orgel mit zwei Manualen zur Verfügung stand. Ist dies der Fall gewesen, so muss es sich um eine Zeit nach der Entstehung von Op. IV gehandelt haben – vielleicht für *Saul*, oder für das Konzert Op. VII Nr. 1, oder für eine (spätere?) Fassung von Op. IV Nr. 3 (erster Satz). In allen diesen Fällen hätte ein aus Mitteldeutschland kommender Organist ohne weiteres vorausgesetzt, dass zu den zwei Manualen auch Pedale gehörten. Dass in Händels Aufstellung keine Zungenstimmen vorgesehen waren, erklärt sich aus seinen eigenen Worten: ‚weil sie ständig gestimmt werden müssen, was auf dem Lande sehr umständlich ist,‘ wenn auch nicht im Londoner Westend. Die Bedingung, die Händel in seinem Brief an Jennens stellte, dass nämlich die Stimme des ‚Open Diapason‘ ganz aus Metall sein müsste, bekräftigt die Aussage, die sein Spiel mit tiefen, anhaltenden ‚Diapason‘-Stimmen beschreibt, weil dafür ein guter offener Bass aus Metall unerlässlich ist. Das Instrument, wie es in diesem Klangbild dargestellt wird, ist fast in jeder Hinsicht ganz anders als die kleinen Orgeln, die der Komponist noch aus Deutschland gekannt haben muss[6] – und zwar in Ton der einzelnen Pfeifenreihen, in der Aufstellung im Gebäude, der Akustik des Gebäudes, der Tonhöhe, wie auch in der Stimmung und im Umfang der Orgel – die beiden Orgeltypen hatten also nichts gemeinsam. Der Londoner Theaterorgel sehr viel ähnlicher war das grössere italienische *Positivo*, und es kann kein Zufall sein, dass die Musik in den Sätzen von *Il Trionfo*, so wie sie für die Orgel gesetzt ist, mit der italienischen Klavier- und Orgelmusik verwandt ist, und damit schon das Op. IV vorausnimmt.

Händels Registration muss ebenfalls der italienischen Tradition entsprochen haben, wie bei den Stimmen ‚Open Diapason+Stopped Diapason+Flute‘ in Op. IV Nr. 4, und bei ‚Open Diapason+Principal+Stopped Diapason+Flute‘ in der Orgelstimme für die Ouvertüre zu *Alexander's Feast* (MS Klavierstimme, R.M. 19. a.1). Letzteres deutet darauf hin, dass sogar in den lauten Tuttipassagen keine hoch gestimmten, Pfeifenreihen in Anspruch genommen wurden. Die begrenzten Möglichkeiten der Theaterorgeln war vermutlich der Grund dafür, dass Händel ‚Org. etc et Basson Grosso‘ für die Stimme des Basso continuo im Chor ‚There let the pealing organ blow‘ des *L'Allegro* (MS R.M. 20.d.5) angab. Was er verlangte, war eine deutsche Pedal-Zungenstimme. Die quasi barocken modernen Registrationen, ganz zu schweigen vom Gebrauch völlig untypischer Orgeln, sind ein Beweis für das weitgehende Missverständnis von Enstehungsgeschichte und Gehalt der Orgelkonzerte Händels.

Bei der vorliegenden Ausgabe habe ich mich an Chrysander (*Händel-Gesellschaft* 28) und Matthäi (*Hällische Händel-Ausgabe* IV/2) gehalten, und mich auf die MS Partituren und die Erstausgaben der gedruckten Stimmen berufen, die ich aber sorgfältiger zum Vergleich herangezogen habe, als die

---

[6] Vgl. z.B. P. Williams, 'A newly restored Handel Organ, *Musical Times*, 1606 (1976) S. 1031 33.

Herausgeber früherer Ausgaben. Die Reihenfolge der Erstausgabe von Walsh habe ich beibehalten, obwohl es wahrscheinlicher ist, dass diese Konzerte in der Reihenfolge 3–2–5–4–6–1 komponiert worden sind. Vermutlich ist der Komponist mit der Anordnung der Werke, so wie sie gedruckt wurden, einverstanden gewesen. In Op. VII bestehen oft Zweifel über (a) den Inhalt aller Konzerte, (b) die Reihenfolge der Sätze, (c) die Instrumentierung der Bässe, (d) die Instrumentierung der Bläser und Streicher, (e) den Stil, Typ und die Länge der *ad lib.* Solo-Passagen oder –Sätze für die Orgel. Das ist in Op. IV selten der Fall, obwohl es gewisse rätselhafte *ad lib.* Hinweise und zweifelhafte Stellen in der Instrumentation für Bläser gibt. Jeder Satz ist in der Stimme des Basses beziffert, aber wer die Stimmen beziffert hat, und weshalb der Bass der Orgel auch in der von Walsh herausgegebenen Klavierstimme in gewissen Sätzen beziffert ist, bleibt unklar. Vielleicht wurden nur in diesen Sätzen Harmonien, oder wenigstens eine dritte Stimme, hinzugefügt. Möglicherweise wurden sie in *allen* Sätzen, besonders den langsamen, hinzugefügt, wenn sie geeignet oder diskret genug schienen. Vielleicht ist die Bezifferung als ein Beweis für den Gebrauch eines zweiten Klavierinstruments zu nehmen, das für die Rolle des Continuo bestimmt war. Schliesslich diente sie vielleicht nur als Hinweis auf die Harmonien, die durch die anderen Stimmen gegeben waren, oder sich durch sie ergaben. Von allen diesen Möglichkeiten ist die erste die letzte die wahrscheinlichste. Da aber der Bass im Orchester gewöhnlich gleichfalls beziffert war, könnte das als weiterer Beweis dafür gelten, dass ein zweites Klavierinstrument verlangt wurde. Allerdings sollte man bedenken, dass damals solche Bezifferungen oft und anscheinend gern angegeben wurden, nur um die Harmonien anzuzeigen, die in den anderen Stimmen enthalten waren, oder sich aus ihnen ergaben. Wie dem auch sei, die Instrumentation in Nr. 4 und 6 (vgl. die Anmerkungen zu diesen Konzerten) beweist, dass der Komponist im ersten dieser Konzerte ein Continuo-Cembalo, und im zweiten eine Continuo-Orgel verlangt hat. Die gedruckte Solostimme enthält, ausser der eigentlichen Solostimme, noch einen Auszug der Ritornellomusik auf zwei Systemen (als ,tutti' bezeichnet), und die ,senza Org.' Passagen. Einige Teile und Sätze sind in der Solostimme beziffert, andere nicht. Das beruht wahrscheinlich mehr auf der Art, wie der Kupferstecher seine Vorlage benutzt (oder interpretiert) hat, als auf einem grunsätzlichen Prinzip des Komponisten.

Die vorliegende Ausgabe hat Mr Anthony Hicks, der mir viele nützliche und wertvolle Ratschläge gegeben hat, viel zu verdanken, sowie Dr William Gudger, der mir freundlicherweise seine Abhandlung 'The Organ Concertos of Handel' (Yale, 1973) zur Verfügung gestellt hat, und Mr Brian Bowen, der die Ausgabe für die Drucklegung eingerichtet hat.

Peter Williams, 1978
Deutsche Übersetzung Stefan de Haan

Organ Concerto Op. IV No. 2 in B flat major

The concerto was probably written early in 1735, as one of the 'new' concertos advertised for the Covent Garden oratorio season: perhaps the 'first Concerto in the Oratorio of Esther' advertised for the performances of *Deborah* (26 March 1735) and *Athalia* (1 April 1735), hence its last movement becoming known as the 'minuet in Esther'. The one extant autograph copy of the whole concerto (see below) leaves the possibility that the opening movement was not composed for or as an organ concerto, since it has its own name ('Sinfonia') and was originally written out as a simple four-stave score without organ part.

Editorial notes

Sources used for this edition are as follows:

A **British Library King's Ms 317, f1–10,** autograph of the complete concerto. The organ part to the first movement ('Sinfonia', 'a tempo ordinario e staccato') was written in by J. C. Smith the Elder.

B **British Library Egerton Ms 2945, f1–8'** copy of complete concerto in the hand of J. C. Smith the Elder, headed 'Concerto 1mo'

C **Cambridge, Fitzwilliam Museum, Lennard Collection, vol 67,** copy of complete concerto in the hand of a copyist in the Smith circle, headed 'Concerto ... 2d (index)

D **Manchester, Public Library, Flower Collection Ms 130 HD 4, vol 84,** copy of complete concerto, headed 'Concerto 1'

E **First edition of parts and keyboard score** (solo part with two-stave reduction of tuttis) by Walsh (1738), entitled *Six Concertos for the Harpsicord or Organ* (solo part entitled *Six Concertos for the Organ and Harpsichord*), Op. IV. Parts are: Violino Primo, Violino Secondo, Viola, Violoncello, Violino Primo Ripieno, Violino Secondo Ripieno, Basso Ripieno, Hautboy Primo & Secondo (single part); the 'Ripieno' parts play only in the *forte* passages, with the wind.

The present edition regularizes the *p/f* signs, giving them to all appropriate parts; none of the sources is consistent in this respect. In the case of ornaments, the edition follows source A rather than E, although some extra ornaments are supplied in square brackets when authorized by analogy or by the other ms sources. The bass-figures are from the Basso ripieno part (**E**).

1 Entitled 'Sinfonia' in **A**; *e staccato* omitted in **B** and **C**. Org part added in A by copyist, but there in other ms sources. In **A, B, C** and **D** the Ob II doubles Vl II, in **E** the Vl I. In **E** Org has extra ornaments, mostly first-beat mordents; the authority for these is unknown.

    1 The wedge-sign **▼** is above the top stave only in **A**; in **E**, only Ob has it

    12 The printed and ms copies assume that the composer required Obs (and Fg) to play at the cadence

2   9 etc.   The placing of *p* mark in **A** is ambiguous; Vla here is made to agree with Vc (in **E,** marked 'solo' in the analogous b38)

    10 etc.   'Tutti ma pianissimo' in **A** is unlikely to mean 'with bassoon' at this and analogous places

    11, 103   In **A,** the *f* sign seems to be placed over the fourth quaver of the bass, not the second or third. However, the ripieno parts of **E** begin *f* on the third quaver.

    39   Vl I trill found in **A** but not **E** etc

    47–50   Since **A** gives the first and last two of these trills, Chrysander was probably right to add those between (HG 28 p25)

    51–4   Solo phrasing and superscript rhythms from **E,** keyboard part

    59   Neither **A** nor **E** makes it clear where the Basso reduces to *p* Vc

    61–2   Small notes in Org from **E**

    95–7   Vla as in **E**; in **A** it reads:

    96   n4 in **E** (Vl I and Obs) is a dotted crotchet

    113   The placing of the ⌢ and *ad libitum* sign in **A** at this point seems to suggest a cadenza on the $^6_4$. **E** gives the *ad libitum* and in one part (Vl II ripieno) the ⌢.

3   In **A,** the decorative solo for Org seems to have been added to the orchestral or skeletal harmonies; b4 is squeezed into two staves of the Org part, as if b5 already sketched.

    A marked 'senza Haut.[b]'; Ob in **E** marked 'The Adagio after the first Allegro is Tacet'; Basso ripieno in **E** marked 'Adagio Tacet'. Vla of **E** is as in this edition (and HG 28 p29); but the other string parts have rests for four parts, followed by a simple cadence, e.g. Vl I:

    See below, b5. Also, in **E** keyboard part, the left-hand chords are realized.

    1   The *tierces coulées* (not *appoggiature*?) in the solo part are from **E,** not **A,** and are kept here because they are more melodic than most ornaments

    3   No triplet sign in **A**; other copies transcribe either as four semiquavers (**E**) or as a triplet (**B, C**)

4   This bar unclear in **A**, because squeezed on to two lines; the rhythmic interpretation here is as understood by **B**, **C** and **D**

5   The first beat of each orchestral part in the score of **A** has an apparently superfluous crotchet rest above the stave, perhaps to indicate that the tutti enters on the second beat. It is probably this ambiguity that led to the garbled parts of **E**. Also, the Org staves have the superscript rest (understood by **B** and **C** to be an inverted mordent), which may suggest that the whole movement before the final orchestral cadence was or could be an *ad libitum*.

Moreover, in b5 of **A**, above the demisemiquaver run in the right hand is written 'etc', perhaps to indicate that the soloist adds more passage-work between the first and second beats

4   In **A**, the first 12 bars of the solo remain blank staves, but the following 4 bars have a rest written through them

1 etc   The articulation signs in Vl I are taken from **A**; the *spiccato* dots are not in **E**, nor are the slurs over the pairs of quavers in bb5–7 etc. The dots are also omitted in **A** at the later points (e.g. b65ff).

46–51   The figures are confused in **E**, Basso ripieno.

89   *p* from **A**

89–96   In **A**, these bars are written out of place on the following page (97 follows on 88), i.e. were added?

97–100   'Viol' (i.e. senza Ob) is not specified in **A** but was so understood in **E**.

Orgelkonzert Op. IV Nr. 2 in B-Dur

Das Konzert wurde wahrscheinlich Anfang 1735, als eines der ‚neuen' Konzerte geschrieben, die für die Saison von Oratorien in Covent Garden angekündigt waren. Vielleicht war es das ‚erste Konzert im Oratorium Esther', das für die Aufführungen von *Deborah* (26. März 1735) und *Athalia* (1. April 1735) angezeigt wurden, weshalb der letzte Satz als ‚Menuett in Esther' bekannt geworden ist. Aus dem einzigen erhaltenen Autographexemplar des ganzen Konzerts ergibt sich die Möglichkeit, dass der erste Satz nicht für ein Orgelkonzert komponiert worden ist, da er seinen eigenen Titel hat (‚Sinfonia'), und ursprünglich als eine einfache Partitur auf vier Systemen ohne Orgel ausgeschrieben wurde.

Organ Concerto Op.4 No.2

G.F. Handel
1685-1759

2

4

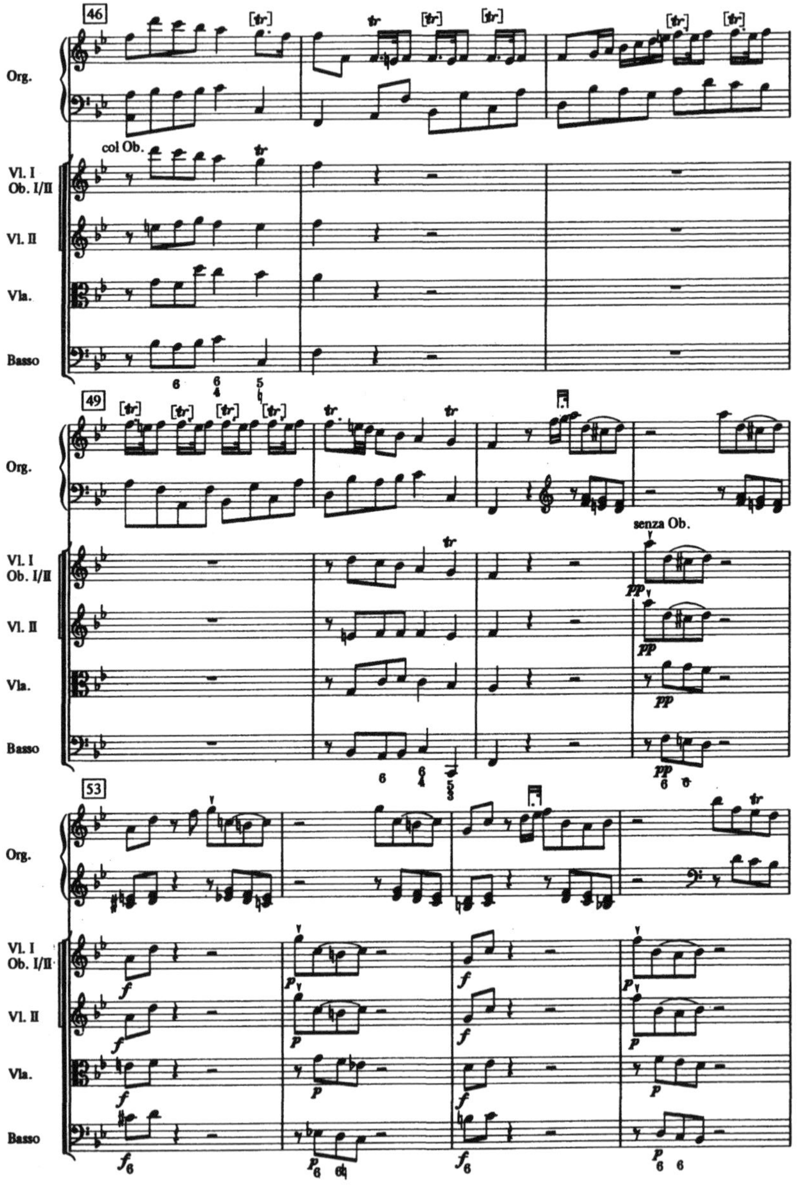
46
Org.
col Ob.
Vl. I
Ob. I/II
Vl. II
Vla.
Basso
49
senza Ob.
53

8

10

EE 6673